Treat Me Right!

Kids Talk About Respect

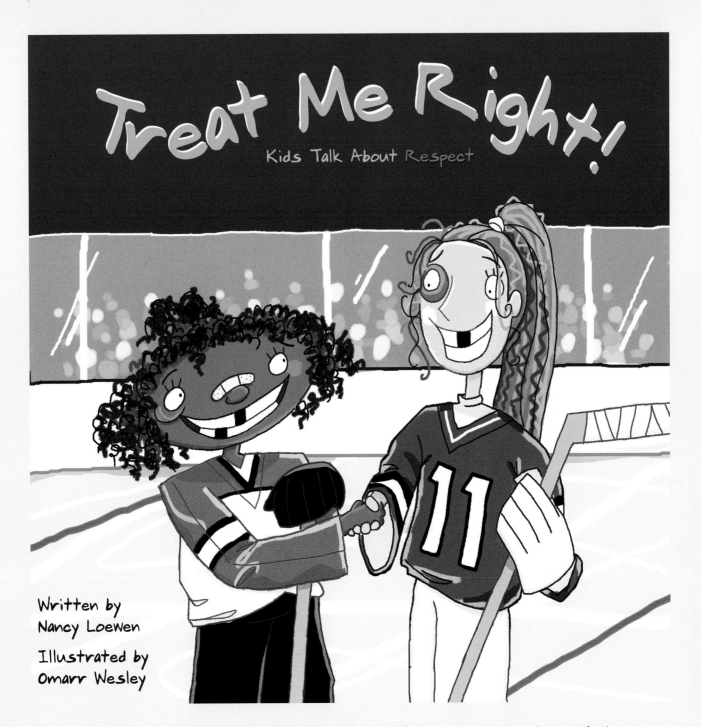

Written by
Nancy Loewen

Illustrated by
Omarr Wesley

Content Advisor: Lorraine O. Moore, Ph.D., Educational Psychology

Reading Advisor: Lauren A. Liang, M.A., Literacy Education, University of Minnesota

PICTURE WINDOW BOOKS
Minneapolis, Minnesota

Editor: Nadia Higgins
Designer: Thomas Emery
Page production: Picture Window Books
The illustrations in this book were prepared digitally.

Picture Window Books
5115 Excelsior Boulevard
Suite 232
Minneapolis, MN 55416
1-877-845-8392
www.picturewindowbooks.com

Printed in the United States of America.
1 2 3 4 5 6 08 07 06 05 04 03

Library of Congress Cataloging-in-Publication Data
Loewen, Nancy, 1964–
  Treat me right! : kids talk about respect / written by Nancy Loewen ; illustrated by Omarr Wesley.
     p. cm. Includes index.
  Summary: Information about various ways of showing respect for others, for property, and for oneself are presented in the form of an advice column.
   ISBN 1-4048-0034-4 (library binding : alk. paper)
   1. Respect—Juvenile literature. [1. Respect.] I. Wesley, Omarr, ill. II. Title.
   BJ1533.R4 L64 2003
   179'.9—dc21
                                                                    2002005891

To my children,
Louis and Helena—
always my best teachers

Hey, what's happening? I'm Frank B. Wize, advice columnist for kids. I'm not famous like Dear Abby or anything (at least not yet!), but I'm 13, so I know a few things. Like, don't eat a marshmallow-jelly-and-banana sandwich before you go on the Tilt 'n' Spin. And if you need to know the difference between a newt, a salamander, and a lizard, I'm your man.

My friends also say that I'm good at helping them with their problems. I guess that's what got me into this advice-column thing in the first place.

Today I'll be looking at letters about respect. It's kind of tough to put into words, but respect is about taking people seriously. It's about being polite. It's about treating them the way you would want them to treat you. You can also show respect to things and places. We'll figure it out some more as we go.

Sincerely,

Frank B. Wize

Hello, Frank.

This new kid moved into our neighborhood. He's from a different country, and he doesn't speak English very well. Some other kids are calling him names and making fun of his clothes. I wish they'd stop it. What can I do?

Jonathan

Dear Jonathan:

Yeah, this is a tough one. It's like me and my friend Yong. He's from Laos. When he first started coming to school, some other kids made fun of him. I didn't join in, but I didn't stand up to them, either. I just ignored the whole thing.

But then Yong and I had to do a report together, and we had such a blast. Once, he tried teaching me how to say some things in Hmong, but I couldn't say them right, and he had a laugh attack because I was saying things like, "I want to be a pickle when I grow up" and "Baseballs fill my stomach."

Okay, back to business. What can you do about the new kid? Well, you can't really MAKE the other kids act better, but you can be nice yourself. You can say hello, ask the new kid questions, show him around. If you do this, do you know what you're really doing? You're showing him respect. You're letting him know that he has a place in your neighborhood.

Yeah, the other kids might tease you at first. But maybe when they see you acting normal with the new kid, they'll get their act together, too. Sometimes all it takes is one kid doing the right thing to change a whole neighborhood.

Thanks for writing, and good luck!

8

Frank B. Wize

Dear Frank:

I have a friend at school who thinks it's fun to dump the sand from his shoes into the water fountain. He says he's just joking around, but this kind of stuff makes me feel really nervous. I wish I could get him to stop. Do you have any suggestions?

Sidekick Sam

10

Dear Sidekick:

I knew a kid who got caught writing on the bathroom walls at school. Not once, but twice. His parents were soooo mad. He had to stay after school for a whole week to scrub off what he'd done. Then, get this: his parents made him volunteer as the custodian's assistant. He was the custodian's total slave one lunch period a week for three months.

That sounds like a big-time punishment, but, man, it really worked. I heard him tell some kids he wouldn't write on another wall even if he was using invisible ink.

What can you tell your friend? I think your best bet would be to ignore him. Tell him you've got better things to do, and then just walk away. Maybe he'll get the message that messing with school property is a huge waste of everyone's time.

If my dad were writing this column, he'd grumble that it's a waste of his tax dollars, too. After all, who pays for public schools? Everyone does. And the more money that's spent on cleaning up bathroom walls and fixing water fountains, the less money there is for fun things like field trips and sports. Try telling your friend that.

And if he doesn't stop, I think it would be okay to tell your teacher or parents or someone. Sometimes kids (and grown-ups, too) do dumb things when they've got problems they don't know how to deal with. Maybe he needs help.

Good luck!

Frank B. Wize

Help me, Frank!

I didn't really want to do it, but Mandy dared me to, and I didn't want her to think I was a chicken and—well—I took a candy bar and some lip gloss from the drugstore. No one saw me, but I still feel like everybody's looking at me all the time. Do you think I'll have to go to jail?

Guilty Grace

Dear Guilty:

I hate to admit it, but I shoplifted once, too. It was at Toys4U. Toby G. dared me to steal a Super Whirly Thingamajig. I didn't want him to think I was a wimp, so I did it. I started feeling really weird right away. Every time I looked at the Thingamajig, I got this whirly feeling in my stomach. Finally I told my dad. He made me go to the store manager to apologize and pay up. That was one of the hardest things I've ever done, but it made that sick feeling go away.

You know what else? Almost as soon as I had that Thingamajig in my hands, I started changing my mind about Toby. That kid was bad news. Friends respect each other. They don't try to get each other to do things they know are wrong.

So, it looks like you'll probably have to 'fess up, Grace. You're lucky that you're too young for jail. But there's a good chance you'll be grounded for a little while.

Take care,

Frank B. Wize

15

Frank, Hi.

What's up with shaking hands with the other team after our hockey games? One minute we're playing against each other as hard as we can, and the next minute we're supposed to be all nicey-nicey. That bugs me.

Out of Sorts in Sports

Dear Out of Sorts:

I hear you. It's not so bad when you win, but it's the worst after getting crushed. You sure don't want to be a sore loser, though. A kid on my brother's baseball team used to cough into his hand—even wipe his nose!— before the team handshake. How uncool is THAT?

In sports you want to try to win. But you've also got to show respect to the kids you're playing against. (Even if they're no good at all!) When you shake hands, or do high fives or whatever, it's like you're saying, "Thanks for taking the time to be here." You're reminding each other that it IS just a game. I mean, it's not life-and-death stuff we're talking about here, even if it feels like that sometimes.

So the next time you go through that line, tell yourself that it's not about winning or losing, and it's not even about being nice. It's about respect. And that's why the pros do it, too.

Bye,

Frank B. Wize

Dear Frank:

My sister has a diary that she's always writing in, and she spazzes out if I even get near it. What's with her?

Tempted to Peek

Dear Tempted:

I have a friend, Reid, whose sister is so worried about someone reading her diary, she has THREE locks for it, and she wears the keys around her neck, even in the bathtub. (Reid says her neck is starting to turn a little green.)

Sisters and diaries are a mystery to me, but I think what you're really asking about is privacy. See, if something is private, that means it's your own personal business. It's up to you if you want to tell other people about it or not. People get along better if they respect each other's privacy. Like, if a door is closed, you need to knock first. You don't just go barging in. Or if someone's on the phone, you don't try to listen in.

It doesn't really matter what's in the diary. The thing is, it belongs to her and no one else. Think how you'd feel if she snooped through your backpack or showed your friends that old teddy bear you still keep around.

Plus, I bet you can find tons of other things to tease her about, even without that diary.

Frank B. Wize

19

Hi, Frank.

Yesterday my dad took me and my friends to see the new Star Squabbles movie. It was great! But now I'm in big trouble. See, Jason started this popcorn fight right as I was taking a huge sip of my grape soda. He made me laugh so hard I ended up spraying the guy in front of me. Now my dad's not going to let me go to any more movies for two whole months. Does that seem fair to you?

Miffed in Minneapolis

Dear Miffed:

It's true, grown-ups tend to get hung up on how kids act in public. I get a lot of letters about that. One kid actually CLAPPED when his sister burped at a school pageant. I think he was grounded for something like two years.

Anyway, you know what it's like when you're watching your favorite TV show, and your sister decides to do headstands right in front of the TV? That's what it was like for your dad and the other people at the movie. I know you didn't MEAN to be disrespectful. You were just having so much fun you were in your own little world. And that's a problem, because the first step in showing respect is to pay attention. You've got to really think about how others might be feeling. I think that's what your dad is getting at.

The good news is, I'm pretty sure your two months will be up by the time the new Galaxy Avengers movie comes out.

Frank B. Wize

21

Hi, Frank.

Why do I have to call my teachers Mr. and Mrs. and Ms.? Why is it okay to call my mom's friend Betty, but my aunt gets mad when people use her first name? And when do you use Sir and Ma'am? I'll never figure it out!

Just Call Me Bob

Dear Bob:

You, me, and the rest of the world! I talked to my teacher about your question, and she agreed that this name stuff is confusing. But she explained things really well, so I think I can help you.

See, those big "M" words—Mr., Mrs., Ms., and Miss—are words that show respect. You use them for most grown-ups. But what you call someone also has to do with how well you KNOW someone. A family friend who's always hanging around is different from someone you've just met, or someone you don't see very often.

Here's the bottom line. Use the "M" words unless that person tells you not to. Then it's okay. And use Ma'am and Sir when you're talking to grown-ups that you don't know. I called my new accordion teacher Ma'am for three weeks, until I finally got it down that her name was Mrs. Truenbach-Tykwinski. (Now I just call her Mrs. T.)

Frank B. Wize

24

Dear Frank:

Sometimes when we go to the park, I forget to put my empty juice box in the garbage. Sometimes I spit my gum out the car window. My sister has a cow when I do things like this, but I don't see what the big deal is.

Karl

Dear Karl:

My little brother, Ben, has these friends who come over sometimes. They're twins nicknamed Dodger and Quick Toes, and let me tell you, those kids are totally wild. By the time they're ready to leave, the floor is covered in candy wrappers and mud and broken toys. After their last visit, Mom said that if Ben wants to play with these guys, it's got to be at THEIR house.

It's the same thing with the park. If you litter, or wreck the playground equipment, it's like you're messing up someone's home—because, really, parks belong to everybody.

Plus, there's the whole idea of how lots of little things add up. Say you go to the park once a week. Every time you go, you leave a juice box on the ground. After a year, you'd have left 52 juice boxes. Now, suppose 40 kids go to the park once a week and do the same thing. After a year, if no one ever came to clean it up, your park would be littered with 2,080 juice boxes! So take, like, two seconds and throw your garbage in the trash. It's a little thing, but it shows respect for our environment and other people. Then you can tell your sister to chill out.

Frank B. Wize

Well, this was kind of fun, huh? Thanks for all your great letters. But I've still got some more to say (when don't I?), so don't leave me now.

Dear Frank:

I spend a lot of time reading. Last month I won the school read-a-thon, and now some kids are calling me names like Book Brain and Librarian's Pet. Can you help me?

Lloyd

Dear Lloyd:

Kids sure can be cruel. When I won the liverwurst-eating contest at the fair, I was called Liver Lips for a whole month.

I showed your letter to my grandpa, and he thought your letter was about self-respect. That means that you know inside that you matter. It's like with me. Not everyone thinks that being an advice columnist is cool. Sometimes kids tease me. It bothers me a little, but then I think—well, this is who I am. I'm not going to stop being who I am just because some kids (who don't really know me) think I'm weird.

My advice is, ignore those kids and keep on reading. Be true to yourself, Book Brain!

Frank B. Wize

Don't groan. This quiz'll be more fun than the ones you take in school, I promise.

1. **If you don't know a grown-up's name, you should call them:**

   A. Cupcake.
   B. Ma'am or Sir.
   C. Hey, you!

2. **Respect:**

   A. is the name of that perfume your mom wants for her birthday.
   B. isn't anything a kid needs to think about.
   C. means to treat other people like they have a place in the world.

3. **Messing up public property on purpose:**

   A. builds up your muscles.
   B. is a bad idea, because it takes time and money away from better things.
   C. shows everyone how cool you are.

4. **Shaking hands with the other team after the game:**

   A. is only for losers.
   B. will bring you seven years of bad luck.
   C. is a good way to show them respect.

5. **At a movie or a play or something like that, it's a good idea to:**

   A. be quiet and at least pretend to listen.
   B. take off your shoe and scratch that itchy spot on your foot.
   C. make faces at the people saying, "Ssshh!"

6. If you respect yourself:

A. you act like you're better than everyone else.
B. you believe that you matter.
C. you eat a lot of liverwurst sandwiches.

7. If people are different from you, you should:

A. pretend they're invisible.
B. watch them closely, take notes, and beam up your report to the Mother Ship.
C. get over it! After all, do you know any two people who are EXACTLY alike?

8. Shoplifting is:

A. stealing.
B. a job for Superman. Who else could lift a shop?
C. okay as long as no one catches you.

9. Privacy is about:

A. keeping some things to yourself, or sharing them with just a few people.
B. not bugging people when they're in the bathroom.
C. minding your own beeswax.
D. all of the above.

10. If you want to show respect for someone, you've got to start by:

A. washing their car or bike.
B. paying attention.
C. copying everything they do.

Answer Key:

1-B, 2-C, 3-B, 4-C, 5-A, 6-B, 7-C, 8-A, 9-D, 10-B

From My Personal Hero File: Rosa Parks

You know, no matter how awesomely terrific an advice column is, sometimes a story from history is an even better way to get across a big idea like respect. And have I got a story for you.

Rosa Parks was a black woman who helped change the world by doing one simple thing. No, she didn't invent a tooth-flossing machine or an automatic peanut-butter spreader, and she didn't send the first iguana into outer space. She sat on a bus. That's it! But what she did marked the start of the Civil Rights Movement.

The Civil Rights Movement is about all people being treated fairly. See, when Rosa Parks sat on that bus, black people couldn't go to the same schools or restaurants as white people. They weren't even allowed to drink water from the same fountains. And when it came to city buses, the black people had to ride in the back. If there wasn't enough room in the front of the bus for all the white people, the black people had to give up their seats. Can you believe it?!

On December 1, 1955, in Montgomery, Alabama, Rosa Parks was riding a bus home after a long day's work as a seamstress. The bus was full, and a white man asked for her seat. Now, Rosa would have gladly given her seat to someone who really needed it, but she didn't think she should have to give it up just because she was black and the man was white. And suddenly she knew what she had to do. Enough was enough! She was going to stand up for what she believed, even if she had to sit down to do it. So that's what she did. She was arrested and put on trial. Eventually the Supreme Court (the most important court in the United States) said that the law that made black people sit in the back was illegal. It was a huge victory for the Civil Rights Movement, and the beginning of some real change in this country.

I just love this story. It's about freedom and courage, but you know what else? I think it's got a lot to do with respect, too. See, Rosa Parks respected herself. She knew she deserved better than what she was getting, and she did something about it. And it wasn't just about her. It was about ALL the people who deserved to be respected as equal people. Cool, huh?

Words to Know

Here are some of my favorite words and expressions from today's column. Use 'em. They'll make you sound really smart.

advice column—what you just read. It's a feature, usually in a newspaper, with letters from people with problems and answers from some smart person who tells them what to do.

diary—a kind of notebook where people write about things that happen in their lives. It's neat, because then someday they can look back and see that on June 3rd they ate three bowls of LoopyNuts for breakfast. Or that on Thursday, October 26th, they got an honorable mention in the all-state science fair. It's hard to believe, but if you don't write down things like that, you might actually forget them.

Laos—a country in southeast Asia. Hmong (pronounced *MUNG*) is the name of that country's language.

liverwurst—sausage that's made out of liver. Don't ask me what liver is. I don't want to go there.

lizard—a reptile with four legs, a long tail, and a scaly body

newt—a little salamander with stubby little legs and a long tail

public—having to do with people in general. A public place is one where everyone can go, like a shopping mall or a baseball stadium. Public is the opposite of private.

respect—to respect someone is to show consideration for that person—to take them seriously, maybe even admire them. And don't forget, you can respect things and places, too.

salamander—an animal that looks like a small lizard, but it's not. (See, I told you that I knew the difference between a lizard, a newt, and a salamander.) A lizard is a kind of reptile. A salamander is a kind of amphibian. And a newt is a kind of salamander. And if you don't know the difference between a reptile and an amphibian, go look it up in a real dictionary. I'm on a deadline.

self-respect—a word that's like respect, only it's directed inward, to yourself. You've got to show consideration for yourself and take yourself seriously. And, yeah, it's even okay to admire yourself—just don't overdo it!

tax dollars—You know how when you buy a toy or something, you usually have to pay a little more than the toy actually costs? That extra money is a tax. People also pay taxes on the money they earn and on their homes. That's the money that the government uses for things like fixing the broken seesaw at the park, or paying the band teacher at school, or sending off a space shuttle.

To Learn More

At the Library

Gainer, Cindy. *I'm Like You, You're Like Me: A Child's Book About Understanding and Celebrating Each Other.* Minneapolis: Free Spirit, 1998.

Kindersley, Barnabas and Anabel. *Children Just Like Me*. New York: Dorling Kindersley, 1995.

Raatma, Lucia. *Self-Respect.* Mankato, Minn.: Bridgestone Books, 2002.

On the Web

KidsHealth
http://www.kidshealth.org/kid
For answers to kids' common questions about growing up

FirstGov
http://www.kids.gov
For links to hundreds of kid-friendly government sites

Want to learn more about respect? Visit FACT HOUND at *http://www.facthound.com*.

Index